WAR

The Indian Army

ISSUED FORTNIGHTLY BY THE

ARMY BUREAU OF CURRENT AFFAIRS

———— Not to be Published ————

No. 26   September 5th, 1942

INDIA *during the* SECOND WORLD WAR

Articles from the Army Bureau of Current Affairs WAR and CURRENT AFFAIRS series, June 1942 to December 1945

CAPTAIN PETER WRIGHT
COLONEL D. H. COLE
SIR STAFFORD CRIPPS

 BooksUlster

First published by the Army Bureau of Current Affairs 1942-45.
This compilation published by Books Ulster in 2016.

Typographical arrangement © Books Ulster

ISBN: 978-1-910375-47-1

Cover: The cover features the post-independence flag of India with men of the 4th Indian Division (centre front) holding a captured German flag at Sidi Omar, North Africa

CONTENTS

CONTENTS

CURRENT AFFAIRS
No. 19, June 6th, 1942

BEAR IN MIND

THIS bulletin is about India. When you have read it, come back to this page and digest a few further considerations before discussing the topic with your men. If you are to have an honest and useful discussion on India you must realise that most Indians (as Sir Stafford Cripps found) take a different view of the Indian question from ours. When your men begin asking questions you may find it well to remind them of such matters as the following:—

1. WE ARE "FOREIGNERS" TO THE INDIANS

We have given India many benefits—health services, education, communications, etc.—yet many millions of Indians have scarcely seen an Englishman. All they know about us is that we originally came to India for our own benefit, not theirs; and it takes many generations of good trusteeship before that sense of antagonism is forgotten.

2. HOW FAR DO RELIGIOUS DIFFERENCES DIVIDE THE INDIANS?

This bulletin gives the British answer. But the Indians say we exaggerate on this point, and that they are more concerned about raising their standard of living than about anything else. They also assert that it is the party leaders and not the rank and file who stress religious differences. (But it is the leaders, of course, with whom our leaders have to deal.)

3. THAT WORD "DOMINION"

The Indians don't like it, and say they prefer the word "independence." They say that they have been hearing "dominion" ever since the last war, and nothing has come of it. We haven't sufficiently won their confidence in our good faith. Remember that other nations in the British Commonwealth used to feel the same, and that it's no good getting impatient or Ill-tempered with people who don't yet see the matter as we do.

4. COULD INDIA EXIST IF IT WERE SPLIT?

Mr. Jinnah, exponent of Pakistan, says it could. But others say no. And they use as a parallel the fact that when, in the U.S.A. in the early '60s, the South wanted to break away, the North went to war to stop it. Remember, though, if you quote this, that there's seldom any such thing as a historic parallel. Time marches on.

5. THE DEFENCE QUESTION

We say that our recent proposals would have given the Indians control of their defence. But they took the view that they were still answerable to the British Viceroy rather than to their own people. They wanted to feel "India is now ours; get together to save our independence."

6. THE CRIPPS MISSION

Although we still haven't got a settlement we have got farther towards one than ever before. Both "sides" are learning a lot about each other; and the slogan for all men of good will should be "Next time does it."

India Faces Total War

The Indian scene and the events leading up to Sir Stafford Cripps's mission to India

By Colonel D. H. COLE, M.B.E.

1. The Hour of Decision

INDIA faces total war. The enemy is 30 miles from the border of its most easterly province, Assam. Indian ports and coastal traffic in the Bay of Bengal have been attacked by air; the Japanese fleet is temporarily in command of some of the ocean approaches to Madras, Vizagapatam and Calcutta, the trio of important ports on the east coast of India; the Japanese army has a central position in Burma, Malaya, Siam and the Netherlands East Indies from which to make its next move. Will that move be towards Australia? Or China? Or Ceylon? Or India? Australia—to capture or neutralise the only remaining repair bases in the Western Pacific which the Allies can use as a pivot for a counter-offensive; China—to liquidate that seemingly endless and expensive adventure which began in 1937; Ceylon—to hold the central base in the Indian Ocean. All these are attractive, most of all the last. But still more inviting is the superb prize of India; the very emblem of British wealth, power and dominion; the keystone of the Indian Ocean. India prostrate would open the way towards the flanks of the British and Russian armies in the Middle East and Caucasus and towards a junction of German and Japanese forces. The rewards would be immense. If such a plan is to succeed it must be carried out quickly before the growing forces of democracy can have time to prevent it. It could only succeed if India failed to play its full part in the struggle. This, in turn, would depend on the unity of purpose and determination existing throughout all its peoples as well as on the strength of its fighting forces and its industrial mobilisation. For in total war it is the aggregate of everyone's will and effort which counts.

2. The Indian Scene

1. Size and Variety of Races, etc.

India cannot be compared with a European nation. It is as large as the whole continent of Europe excluding Russia. Cut out of a map of the world and superimposed on Europe so that its most southerly point is placed on Sicily, its most northerly point would lie in Norway and it would stretch west and east from the Atlantic coast of Ireland to the borders of Russia. Distances are correspondingly great; road journeys of five or six days by car and train journeys of 36 hours or more are not out of the ordinary, and Calcutta, Bombay and Peshawar are farther from one another than London is from Belgrade. Its people number 389 millions—that is more than twice the population of Soviet Russia, nearly three times that of the United States and one-fifth of the population of the world. This population is not homogeneous in race. There are at least eight distinct racial strains in the make-up of its peoples—some as different from others as the Western European is from the Eastern Asiatic or the Tropical African. Over 220 languages are spoken, some by many millions of people; and variations in local vernaculars run into thousands. No Englishman, and perhaps no Indian, is a sufficient master of languages to travel throughout the length and breadth of the country and make himself understood in every part in its own tongue. The spoken word (as contrasted with the written word) is all-important, for 88 per cent. of the population are illiterate in the sense that they cannot read or write, and the vast masses of the people are dependent for their news and views on what they hear and not on what they read.

2. Agricultural and Backward

It is predominantly an agricultural country. In the aggregate its agricultural wealth is great because of its vast area. But it is unevenly distributed. The alluvial plain of the Ganges and the irrigated plain of the Punjab hold two-thirds of its people and a still larger part of its arable land. Even there and still more so in other parts the wealth is thinly divided and the poverty of the Indian peasant is by European standards incredible. So also is his lack of knowledge of the great outer world and its affairs. It is no exaggeration to say that half the people of India have never seen a newspaper, heard a wireless set, been in a train, watched an aeroplane in the sky or ventured farther from their own villages than 20 miles.

3. Religions

European nations differ widely in many respects but they share, at any rate nominally, the common religious background of the Christian faith. It is not so in India. There, religions in great variety exist side by side, varying from philosophic systems of vast profundity at one end of the scale to the primitive worship of local village deities and crude images at the other. The latest census figures are not available, but the following are approximately correct for the main religious groups:—

Caste Hindus .. .. 240 millions
Depressed or Scheduled Classes (who are within the pale of Hinduism but have no caste) . .. . .50 millions
Mohammedans .. .. .80 millions
Christians (mainly Anglo-Indians). .. ..6 millions
Sikhs.. .. ..5 millions
Others. .. ..8 millions

(a) Hinduism

Hinduism, the religion of the majority, is a comprehensive term much wider and more elastic than Christianity. It embraces the worship of a whole pantheon of gods and goddesses and covers a range of religious practices from the strictest asceticism to the crudest and most primitive observances. But in spite of the variety which it includes within it there is an essential unity. All Hindus believe in the Trinity of Brahma (The Creator), Vishnu (The Preserver) and Shiva (The Destroyer); all ascribe a religious importance (and sanctity) to certain animals such as the cow, the monkey and the peacock. All must—because the cow is sacred—avoid destroying it—hence the millions of useless cattle which roam the plains of India— and abhor beef as a food. All must observe the rules of the caste system in general and of their own caste and sub-caste in particular.

This strange social-religious system of caste, whose origin is unknown, may have been a development of a "herrenvolk" idea among the Indo-Aryan races who swarmed into the plains of northern India in successive waves of migration from Central Asia some three thousand years ago, and thrust southward the original dark-skinned inhabitants. It became an integral part of their religion and of their social system, and to-day there are some 2,000 castes and sub-castes. It is not a mere difference in classes of society, for it has a rigidity and permanence which no social differences elsewhere possess. No effort on a man's part can move him from one caste into another. Birth fixes it for him. He must marry within it; it prescribes his forms of religious ceremonial, his food and often his occupation. If he breaks his caste rules he may suffer the dire punishment of ex-communication.

(b) The "Untouchables"

Outside the pale of caste Hinduism are the "untouchables," numbering some 50 millions. While they may worship the same gods they are denied contact with caste Hindus even in schools, hospitals or temples. They are regarded as unclean by the "caste" Hindu, must live apart in a separate quarter of each town or village, and generally carry out certain occupations, such as laundry work, leather work, sweeping and cleaning, which caste Hindus cannot perform without being contaminated. With the spread of education they are slowly becoming a political force under an able leader, Dr. Ambedkar, a distinguished Bombay lawyer. But, though exceptions can be quoted, and some caste Hindus, like Mr. Gandhi, have lent their influence to remove the stigma of "untouchability" with all that it implies, it still prevails throughout India to-day almost as greatly and rigidly as it did ten centuries ago.

(c) Mohammedans

The Moslem community is the largest and politically most active minority in India. It is most numerous in the north and north-west, and in western Bengal, and outnumbers the Hindus in the provinces of Bengal, the Punjab, Sind and the North-west Frontier. The division between it and the Hindu community is not merely fundamental in religion but rooted in history and accentuated by economic factors. This does not imply that Hindus and Moslems are always in a state of friction or inimical to one another in business or politics. There are many exceptions, as there are to any generalisation about India. Some Mohammedans belong to the predominantly Hindu Congress Party, and its president, Maulana Kalam Azad, is a distinguished Moslem scholar; the North-west Frontier Province, which is almost entirely Mohammedan in population, is Congress in politics; Mohammedans and Hindus serve loyally side by side as comrades in the Indian Army; the two communities, on the whole, live amicably enough together as a rule. But inter-community ("communal") passion is easily set ablaze by some incident which inflames religious, economic or political differences. To say that the British policy in India has stirred up these differences for its own imperialistic ends is mere nonsense. It is only true in so far as the advent of democratic forms of government has made these differences more acute. They, unfortunately, exist and are a factor which cannot be ignored in India's present situation and future development.

In religion the Moslem believes in one God and one prophet, and in the social equality of mankind—and is thus diametrically opposed to the polytheism and caste system of Hinduism. He claims descent—not always correctly—from Mohammedan invaders who swept through the passes of the North-west Frontier, conquered most of India and established the great Mogul Empire which dominated most of the country for 300 years. He thus regards himself as the descendant of warrior peoples who once held sway over the more numerous Hindus, and as the heir of a great tradition. Economically, he is more frequently an agriculturist than a merchant, is rarely wealthy, and is not so aware of the advantages of an educational system which has been the main door to official advancement. Islam to him is wider than India, and the educated Moslem feels that he is part of a community embracing all the Mohammedan lands beyond its borders.

In the political scene these differences are represented by the Congress party with its mainly Hindu adherents and leaders, such as Mr. Gandhi and Pandit Jawaharlal Nehru, and the Moslem League, whose president is Mr. M. A. Jinnah. Congress claims to speak with the voice of the majority and insists that the majority voice should prevail. The Moslem League and, indeed, all other minorities, reject any system which would place them in permanent subjection in a government of India to a Congress or Hindu majority.

3. The Political Framework

1. British India and the Indian States

To understand the political scene one further complication must be described. The term "India" includes two completely different types of territorial division and of government. The larger part—with more than half of the area and three-quarters of the population—is British India, divided into eleven Provinces, each of which, by the Government of India Act of 1935, was granted a very full measure of provincial autonomy on democratic lines, subject to certain safeguards in respect of law and order, minorities and public security. The remainder consists of the India of the Princes—comprising nearly 600 States, some as large as European countries, some only a few acres in extent. These are not British territory. Their rulers have powers and privileges guaranteed to them by Treaty or Sanad, subject to the general paramountcy of the British crown. Their forms of government are generally benevolently autocratic. The Government of India Act which conferred wide powers of Provincial autonomy on British India left open a door for an eventual Federation of British India and the Indian States on some basis which would safeguard the treaty rights of the Princes, but this—like many other things—had not been attained when war broke out.

2. The Central Government (The Government of India)

The Government of India Act of 1935 granted to the Provinces of British India the power to set up ministerial government responsible to legislatures elected on a much more extended franchise. This marked an important advance towards responsible self-government for India as a whole, which, as early as 1917, had been announced as the ultimate goal. But no equal advance could be made in the Central Government of India pending the conclusion with the State of the negotiations to set up a Federal Government or Legislature. The existing Central Government temporarily continued under the Act. It had, it was true, two houses of Legislature, partly elected and partly nominated, but the executive power remained in the hands of the Governor-General and an Executive Council consisting of certain European officials such as the Commander-in-Chief as defence member, and a number of Indian members nominated by the Governor-General. The Executive was not responsible to the Legislature, though the latter had one power (freely exercised, it may be said) of surveying and criticising the acts of the executive. The legislative bodies, moreover, were, as their name suggests, the organs for law making, but if they failed to conform with the needs of the Executive the Governor-General had overriding powers to make such laws and ordinances as were necessary.

The situation was intended to be merely transitional. When at least half the more important States would join on terms acceptable to themselves and the Crown, then a Federation of Princes and States would be set up. It was expected that this Federation would in course of time evolve into a "Dominion of India." Unfortunately, as has been said, the prerequisites had not been achieved, and it was clear that the political parties were not content with the Federal plan, when the outbreak of war put an end to the negotiations.

3. Indian Politics 1937–1939

Nevertheless, the Act succeeded better than its opponents had ever believed to be possible. In the four Provinces where there is a Moslem majority, responsible governments were set up and still exist. In the seven remaining Provinces where there was a Congress majority, Congress ministries after some hesitation came into office and remained until November, 1939. Their two years of office was, apart from much useful legislation passed, a valuable educative period for these young governments, and for the Indian Ministers who had to assume responsibilities and bear with criticism.

But the outbreak of war brought this to an end. The Congress Party, though asserting its dislike of Nazism and Fascism as forms of Imperialism, protested against the declaration of India as a belligerent without the consent of the Indian people and demanded the right of self-determination to frame for India, through a constituent assembly and without external interference, a Constitution for India. A little later the All-India Congress Committee stated that "India must be declared an independent nation" and "present application must be given to this status to the largest possible degree." This was quickly followed by a resolution of the Moslem League which welcomed the suspension of the Federal scheme (announced by the Viceroy on September 11th, 1939) for the duration of the war and urged its complete abandonment because "under the guise of parliamentary rule it must result in majority community (viz., Congress) rule." Conversations and conferences pressed on one another day after day, but no unity or any sensible course of action resulted from them. Congress, in effect, demanded majority rule and no exceptions; the Moslem League and other minority bodies demanded that there should be no surrender to the Congress demands; the British Government and the Viceroy strove hard to find some common denominator which would satisfy all Indian party leaders and at the same time do no damage to the vitally important war effort of India. By November the Ministries of the seven Congress Provinces had (some of them unwillingly) resigned on the instructions of the All-India Congress committee, and although in one Province ministerial government has been restored, it has since collapsed—so that the seven Provinces are still administered by their Governors.

4. The Aims of the Chief Parties

For long past, British policy in India has been mainly directed towards inducing Hindus and Moslems to bury the hatchet and work together. Instead of doing this, one unfortunate effect of the advance towards self-government has been to increase rather than lessen the political hostility between them. Congress, led by Mr. Gandhi, Maulana Abdul Kalam Azad and Pandit Nehru, have consistently refused to look at any objective except a system of numerical democracy which, since the Hindus are three to one, would set up a permanent Hindu rule. They are particularly insistent that this should apply to the central government as well as to the provincial governments—a demand which would, if granted, ensure that the central government would always be Hindu and Congress.

The Moslem League retorted with the "Pakistan" scheme. This is a project for cutting the areas with Moslem majorities (whole States and Provinces and bits of Provinces) out of an Indian federation and constituting them into a separate nation—perhaps allied to or even federated with neighbouring Moslem states like Afghanistan. The Congress objections to this are that it would break up a country whose unity is becoming increasingly important and self-evident, that it would leave India without a strategically satisfactory frontier and that it would place large Hindu minorities under Moslem and, perhaps, "foreign" rule.

Though most attention is naturally focused on these two main parties in Indian politics there are other parties and personalities which help to make up the Indian political scene. There is, for instance, the Hindu Mahasabha, orthodox Hindu in composition, but less rigidly doctrinaire and dogmatic in its political ideals than Congress. It stands, like Congress, for complete independence at some time but is willing to accept Dominion status as an instalment. It condemns outright the Pakistan scheme and the British Government for not agreeing to any constitution unless it is approved of by the Moslem minority. On the other hand it is in favour of the expansion of the Indian Army, of compulsory military training in schools, of the recruitment of Hindus and the development of war production.

Then, there are moderate Liberals of the old school who strive to act as honest brokers in bringing the Congress and Moslem parties closer together. In the past it is from this party that most of the Indian members of the Viceroy's Executive Council have been drawn. There is also a strong Anglo-Indian party composed of Indian nationals who have some British or European blood. They are Christian and mainly Roman Catholic, and are generally intensely loyal to the British connection. There are the Sikhs, that warrior community compactly situated in the Punjab where they form the most powerful minority, whose deeds have been famous in many fields of war. Sikhism, their religion, though monotheistic, is nearer in its forms and origin to Hinduism than to Mohammedanism or Christianity. Once the rulers of the Punjab, they are now a minority community in a Moslem governed province. They view the Pakistan scheme with dismay, and look to the British Government to safeguard their rights and property in any Constitution-making which takes place. They, like other minorities, are unwilling to trust their fate to the mere counting of heads. There is, indeed, as yet, in India, little confidence in the vision, statesmanship or spirit of toleration which any of the political parties would exercise over the others if placed in positions of power unchecked by British safeguards.

5. Efforts to Enlist the Co-operation of Indian Leaders in the War Effort

By July, 1941, in spite of the most wholehearted efforts by the Viceroy to induce the Indian political parties to settle their differences and come, in consultation, to some agreement about the future constitution of India, little had been accomplished. Indian party leaders stood aloof from the war effort, each perched on his own political platform. It is an interesting reflection on Indian politics that, nevertheless, the Indian war effort proceeded with a pace which astonished even those who know India and its peoples. Volunteers for the armed forces raised the strength of the Indian Army from 237,000 in 1939 to over one million in July, 1941, and they were still coming forward faster than they could be housed, officered or equipped. The production of war materials kept step with recruiting. India became the headquarters of the Eastern Supply Group which co-ordinated the supply arrangements of all the Allied Forces and countries from the Middle East to the Western Pacific. Its factories and shipyards worked at high pressure and new war industries which had never before been considered possible, sprang up. Nevertheless there is little doubt that the total effort would have been greater if it had had the wholehearted support of Congress and all the other parties. The expansion of the Viceroy's Executive Council in July, 1941, so that it would contain for the first time a majority of Indian non-official members, and the establishment of a National Defence Council, a consultative body consisting of 20 British Indian and nine State representatives, were moves in the direction of associating Indian public men with the war effort. But they went no measurable distance towards satisfying any of the demands of the Congress party, which continued to reiterate in substance its resolution of March, 1940.

"Congress strongly disapproves of Indian troops being made to fight for Great Britain ... neither recruiting nor money rased in India can be regarded as voluntary contributions from India ... Congress declares again that nothing short of complete independence can be accepted."

6. Japan Strikes

This was how matters stood when the events of Sunday, December 7th, 1941, brought total war to the gates of India. The subsequent events need no recapitulation here. They taught in blood and destruction one lesson at least—that victory in total war needs total effort and total resistance to the enemy. Was such possible in an India already in the firing line unless every leader of repute gave all his energy and purpose to the great tasks of educating the Indian peoples in their rôle in the war effort, to the development of its fighting services and its industrial war effort? Nothing less than everything is best for these times. Could the Indian leaders bury their political hatchets, come together, agree on a policy for the present, work for the defence of India in its imminent danger and, above all, settle by agreement among themselves the future status of their own land? It was in the hope that they could do so that the War Cabinet framed proposals which were a businesslike compromise between the various party demands. It was in the spirit that India could arise, if she willed, to this great need and occasion that Sir Stafford Cripps brought those proposals to India.

7. What Had to be Reconciled in These Proposals?

The proposals had to reconcile the following:—

1. *The demands of the Congress Party for a democratic Government throughout India—at the Centre, in the Provinces and in the States, with the right to be completely independent of all connection with Great Britain.*

2. *The demand of the Moslem League to be cut clean out of such a scheme and to have a Moslem State or Federation of Moslem States (Pakistan) embracing all large concentrations of Mohammedans in India.*

3. *The rights of the Indian States whose rulers have treaties or agreements with the British Crown.*

4. *The rights of the many minorities, large or small, articulate or inarticulate.*

5. *The preservation of India from internal disorder while total war is on its threshold, and the avoidance of any course of action which would reduce the war effort.*

My Mission to India

By The Right Hon. Sir STAFFORD CRIPPS, M.P., Lord Privy Seal

IT is with very great pleasure that I take advantage of this opportunity which has been given to me by ABCA to tell the members of the British fighting services something of the Mission to India which I have recently undertaken on behalf of His Majesty's Government. The importance of this Mission will be recognised by you all—especially after you have studied and discussed the informative notes on the background of the Indian situation which form the main sections of this Bulletin.

India is a far-off country, but it is one which occupies a vital position in our war effort. Not only has it become a bastion against the westward advance of Japanese aggression, it has become a test of the sincerity of our claims to be fighting this war for the freedom of mankind. In India the armed forces of the United Nations—America, Britain and India herself—combine to resist the common enemy of civilisation in the east. In India I had the high honour of placing before the leaders of that great country the British Government's far-reaching offer of freedom and self-government.

Why India Asks for Self-government

There is much in the long story of the relations between India and Britain which is open to serious criticism, but there is also a great deal which is admirable, and the whole of the tale is not yet told. The central fact which we British have to face to-day is that the ideas of national freedom and democracy which we brought to India have permeated the educated and politically conscious sections of the great Indian communities and have—naturally enough—engendered a morally irresistible demand for self-government. It was to find the means to satisfy this demand that I went out to India, carrying with me far-reaching proposals which had the unanimous backing of the members of the War Cabinet.

The Task of the Mission

What did the Mission set out to do? The problem with which we were faced was by no means a simple one. We had to reconcile the apparently incompatible views of the Indian Congress Party (predominantly though not entirely Hindu in composition); the Moslem League; the Hindu Mahasaba (an orthodox Hindu party) and other important groups—all of which were united in their demand for self-government, but very divided as to the form which the future Indian constitution should take. We had, in particular, to deal with the claims of the Moslem League that the Moslem provinces of India should form their own independent State—Pakistan—quite separate from the rest of India. We had to find a means of bringing into the new Constitution the Indian States, the rulers of which were Indian Princes, with long-standing treaties or agreements with the British Government. It was essential to make some provision for the protection of Indian minority communities—such as the Sikhs, the Indian Christians, and the Depressed Classes. Above all—with the Japanese at the gates—we had to avoid any action which would impede the defence of India during the critical months which were immediately ahead. This was no light task, as I am sure you will agree, but it was one which had to be undertaken if for no other reason than to show the Indians and the world at large that, in the claiming to be fighting this war not merely to resist aggression but to extend the boundaries of human freedom, we were deadly in earnest.

The British Proposals

What then did our proposals amount to? In the first place, we made it clear beyond all doubt that India should have complete freedom and self-government the moment the war was over and the Indians had framed a new Constitution for their country. The British Government's draft Declaration spoke of India becoming a Dominion of the British Commonwealth of Nations, but it went on to say that the British Government would not "impose any restrictions on the power of the Indian Union to decide in the future its relationship to the other Member States of the British Commonwealth." India would be quite free to leave the Commonwealth if her peoples so decided—just as Canada, South Africa and the other Dominions are free to do to-day. As to the details of the Constitution for the new India, the British Government suggested that a particular form of Constitution-making body should be set up immediately the war came to an end. But it was made perfectly plain that if the Indians themselves agreed upon some alternative plan this would be accepted by us.

In order to overcome the fear of the great Moslem community lest our proposals should put them under the permanent domination of a Hindu majority and rule out the possibility of their ever achieving the goal of a separate Moslem State in India, we suggested that any Indian Provinces which wished to contract out of the proposed Indian Union should be allowed to do so and to form a separate Union of their own—equal in status with the major Indian Union. The ultimate test would be the expressed wish of the majority of the adult male population in the Provinces—that is to say, a plebiscite—though this would not be necessary in most Provinces, where the result in favour of remaining in the Indian Union would be a foregone conclusion.

We do not want to see any break-up of the unity of India, which we regard as one of the great contributions we have made to her future, but unity cannot be imposed on a free nation. For this reason we felt, not only that it was consistent with our promises to the Moslems to give them this opportunity of deciding their own destiny, but also that it would, in fact, make an agreement between Moslems and Hindus to come into a single union much more likely. Our duty was to suggest means whereby the issue could be settled fairly with the least discord—and this I think we were able to do. I do not believe that it would be possible for us to find, under existing circumstances, a fairer solution of the problem. Moreover, I must emphasise that the scheme was no rigid and unchangeable plan, since here again the way was left open to the Indian communities to agree among themselves on a better alternative.

The Indian States and the Minorities

As we were anxious to see an India united and strong in her freedom we made provision also for the participation of the Indian States in the body which we proposed should undertake the task of planning the new Indian Constitution, and for negotiating a revision of the treaties with the rulers so far as this might be required by the new filiation. We believed that this would not only lead to the rulers of these States joining the new Indian Union, but also enable the people of these States to share in the wider and, we hoped, more democratic life of India as a whole. Unfortunately, in my view, representative institutions have not yet developed in the great majority of these States. But it would have been a mistake to exclude them from the scheme on this account. A closer association with democratic India would almost certainly lead to the rapid development of democratic institutions in the States themselves.

Then there was the difficulty of the minority communities who felt that as soon as British rule was withdrawn they would be left at the mercy of one or other of the larger communities—Hindu or Moslem— who, they feared, would not respect their economic or religious interests. It was impossible to ignore the feelings of these minority communities, and we made special provision in our proposals in accordance with the undertakings which British Governments have repeatedly given for the protection of racial and religious minorities. We suggested that these matters should be the subject of a Treaty to be negotiated between His Majesty's Government and the constitution-making body to be signed before the new constitution came into operation.

These proposals naturally led to a great deal of public discussion when I announced them in Delhi.

Indian Criticism

It was not to be expected that there would be a chorus of praise from all sides. Political compromises seldom evoke popular enthusiasm, however wise and statesmanlike. The representatives of Congress did not like our use of the word "Dominion." They objected to the proposal to allow the people of predominantly Moslem Provinces to vote themselves out of the Indian Union if they wished; and some of them would have liked us to abandon our long-standing treaty arrangements with the Indian States at a moment's notice. The Moslems, on the other hand, were disappointed that we had not yielded to their demand for Pakistan—an independent Moslem State.

The minority communities were apprehensive lest the Treaty provisions which we promised to make to safeguard their interests would not give them the protection which they felt they needed. But upon the fundamental and vital point of Indian self-government there was no disagreement. It was universally recognised that the proposals were very far-reaching and that they offered to India the substance of political freedom as soon as hostilities ceased. This is the most vital fact about our Mission, and when the dust of controversy has subsided it will, I believe, be looked back upon as a historic turning point in the relations between our two countries.

Why the Mission Failed

Why, then, you may well ask, did the Mission fail in its immediate objective? Why did the conversations break down? I think it is fair to say that differences of opinion over the long-term proposals which we took to India were not the cause. When all reservations had been made our scheme was recognised to be an honest attempt to find a way through a very complex situation. On this, agreement could have been reached. The breakdown occurred because the leaders of Congress were not satisfied with the proposals which we made for their *immediate* participation in the government, and in the defence, of their country. It was to this issue that I devoted most of my time in Delhi.

Our difficulty here arose from the fact that, although we were anxious to engage the active co-operation of the leaders of all the principal Indian communities in organising resistance against the Japanese, we could not embark on the complicated and lengthy task of re-making the Indian Constitution at such a critical moment. It was something which we were bound to postpone until the immediate menace had been removed. Moreover, we felt we could not, at such a time, throw upon General Wavell, the Commander-in-Chief, the additional task of disentangling the complex arrangements which linked his military responsibilities with the administrative work of the Defence Department of the Government of India.

What we did was to suggest an arrangement whereby the Indian leaders might have immediately entered the Viceroy's Executive Council and taken over all the "Ministerial" posts in the Government, except those of the Viceroy himself and of the Commander-in-Chief. With regard to Defence in the narrow sense of that term, we proposed to create a new Defence Department, with an Indian Minister who would be responsible for some of the functions previously exercised by the Commander-in-Chief, and for some others, including the protection of the civil population in threatened areas, and other important duties. It should be remembered that the control of such matters as war supplies, transport, man-power and finance—all vital for the defence of India—would under our proposals have been placed immediately under the control of leading representatives of the great Indian political parties.

To my great sorrow these interim arrangements—the best it was possible to offer with the Japanese at the gate—were not accepted by the leaders of Congress. They did not go far enough to meet the demand for a completely National Government with full responsibility to be set up at once. Nor do I think a more inclusive offer could have been accepted by the minorities. This being the case I had to return from India without having accomplished my immediate task. But I do not believe that all the results of the Mission are on the debit side. Our intention to give India her freedom has been stated clearly and precisely. Our sincerity in this matter has been demonstrated beyond doubt. And, although the memories of the past are still, perhaps, too strong for complete confidence to have been established, I have the feeling that we have taken a great step forward in winning the friendship of many of the younger elements In India, who are perhaps less influenced by the struggles and bitterness of the past than some of their older colleagues.

Looking back on this historical episode, I feel no regret at the decision of the Government to send me with these proposals to India. I am convinced that the proposals were just and that we have done all that we could in a very difficult situation to bring about a better understanding between our two peoples. It is, in fact, the past exercising its influence upon all parties that has proved too strong for us, and we must now leave the leaven of better understanding to work quietly towards an ultimate and satisfactory solution of the political problem. If we are to do this, let us at all costs forgo the transient satisfaction of blaming others and of encouraging those very antagonisms which have been a major part of our difficulty.

WAR
No. 26, September 5th, 1942

The Indian Army

Written for WAR by an Indian Army Officer, in conjunction with the War Staff of the India Office.

AT a time when the non-co-operation of the politicians makes most of the news from India, it is well to remember the superb co-operation of her soldiers in the war against the world's three principal enemies. Already Indian troops have fought the Italians in Abyssinia and Eritrea, the Germans in Libya and the Japanese in the Far East. Men of the Royal Indian Army Service Corps were in France from the start and were evacuated from the beaches of Dunkirk.

The Indian Army of to-day is the lineal descendant of the armies raised in different parts of India by the trading concern known as the East India Company. There were the armies of the three presidencies, Bengal, Madras and Bombay, each under its own commander. Later, the Punjab Frontier Force was formed, to defend the north-west frontier. In 1903 all these forces were amalgamated by Lord Kitchener into one army.

In 1932 there was a reorganisation. The main features of this were the halving of the Indian cavalry by amalgamating every two regiments into one, and the grouping of infantry units into regiments of five or six battalions, all having the same composition and a common recruit training unit. It may be said in passing that the names of units are nowadays no guide to the origin of the men who compose them.

The Official Rôle

At the outbreak of the present war, the rôles of the army in India had recently been accepted as being:—

(1) The defence of India's sea and land frontiers, including the control of the tribal areas on the north-west frontier.
(2) The maintenance of internal security.
(3) The provision of certain forces equivalent to a division, for the external defence of India.

Complete modernisation had been recommended in 1939 by the Chatfield Committee, and had been accepted. Soon after the outbreak of war it became evident that the army would require to be considerably expanded to meet possible threats and to provide additional formations for service overseas.

The strength of the army in India pre-war was about 220,000 men. Of these, 180,000 comprised the Indian Army, and the remaining 42,000, were British troops. The Indian troops comprised 18 regiments of cavalry, 95 battalions of infantry, 8 mountain artillery regiments, 3 corps of sappers and miners (the Indian equivalent of the Royal Engineers), and all ancillary services.

The Indian Army has now been expanded to over a million, and recruits are coming in at the rate of over 50,000 a month.

The Men Themselves

Now who are the Indian soldiers—the victors of Keren and Sidi Barrani, Damascus and Ambar Alagi? They are men of very differing races and creeds—all volunteers—all regarding the profession of arms as a most honourable one, and practically all yeomen farmers following a family tradition in joining the army. They only come from certain sections of the population, as a large proportion of the inhabitants of India, either through heredity or environment, are unsuited to be soldiers.

A considerable proportion of Indian soldiers comes from the Punjab. It produces the Sikhs (S),* a fighting community in its origin. They are fine and stubborn fighters who will hold a position till all is blue. Sikhs never shave or cut their hair, which they roll in a knot on the top of their heads. The term Punjabi Muselman (P.M.) covers several tribes—they are excellent all-round fighters, can always be relied upon, and provide a very high proportion of the army. Many grow their hair long and cut it in a bob round the nape of the neck. Some tribes are very handsome with clean-cut Grecian features and may be descendants of colonies founded by Alexander the Great.

From the hills come Dogras (D) and Garhwalis (GA)—high caste Hindus. They are small but hardy, and the Garhwalis in particular built up a great reputation in the last war in France. From the Southern Punjab come the Jats (J). They sometimes appear a bit slow and stolid, but are excellent soldiers.

They are Intensely Proud

Rajputana is the home of the Rajputs (R), the direct descendants of the warrior caste of the Aryans who first came to India in 1500 B.C. They are an intensely proud race, inclined to despise everything but the profession of arms. They are particularly fine horsemen, but now their mounts are mechanised.

The Mahratta (M) Cavalry were the bugbear of the British Commanders in the days of John Company, the old East India Company. Their descendants who live in the Bombay Presidency, though now they fight as infantry, have lost none of their ancestors' spirit.

From the north-west frontier and independent tribal territory come Pathans (P), often big men with wheat-coloured complexions. They are brave and cunning fighters.

---

* Letters in brackets denote abbreviations used in map.

The Madrassis (MA) from the province of Madras fought many successful battles under Sir Arthur Wellesley, who later became Duke of Wellington. They have for long done fine service as sappers and miners, and are now being enlisted in large numbers for artillery, infantry and signal units.

Finally, we have the Gurkhas (GU) from the independent

kingdom of Nepal on the north-east frontier. They are small men with Mongolian features, very cheerful and tough fighters. Their particular joy is to get to close quarters with their kukris—deadly broad-bladed curved knives.

It may be asked, "How is an army, consisting of such different races, organised?" Generally speaking, Indian organisation is based on home establishments. The normal system is for a regiment or battalion to be composed of three or four different classes grouped in one squadron or company each. There are, however, a number of what is known as "Class Units," that is, units formed from only one class. Gurkhas, for instance, are invariably formed in class units.

Moslems and Hindus are usually enlisted in the same units. Each keep to their own customs, and have their own feeding arrangements, and their own places of worship, but they get on extremely well together, do duties together, and there is no religious or other friction. The Indian sepoy gets free rations, fuel, uniform, etc., and his basic pay is about Rs.18 per month (about £1 4s.). The rate of living of the Indian people is low, and most of their essential requirements are very cheap.

What About the Officers?

The officering of the Indian Army differs somewhat from that of the British service. There is a class of officer who holds the Viceroy's commission. The platoon in the infantry, the troop in the cavalry, and the equivalent of such units in other arms of the Indian Army are commanded by these Viceroy's commissioned officers.

This grade, to which the best of the non-commissioned officers are promoted, roughly corresponds in status to the warrant officer of the British Army. The grade acts as liaison between the men and the British officers, who cannot have that intimate knowledge of customs, religious sentiment and so on, which is possessed by Indians themselves.

The senior grade, known as subadars in the infantry and risaldars in the cavalry, wear the badges of rank of a lieutenant; the junior grade, known as jemadars, those of a second lieutenant. The senior V.C.O. in the unit is the risaldar- or subadar-major, who, in addition to his other duties, is the confidential adviser of the commanding officer.

Commissioned officers are both British and Indians. They work together side by side in all units of the Indian Army, and, of course, live together in the same mess. British officers and certain Indian officers (see below) hold the same commission as officers of the British Army. The remaining officers hold commissions corresponding to the Dominion commissions held by Canadian, South African, etc. officers. The establishment of commissioned officers in a battalion is 14.

Promotions are made in exactly the same way as in the British Army. British and Indian commissioned officers are treated alike, and are judged by the same standards: when either holds a senior appointment he must have proved his worth, and must continue to do so.

Because of the relatively small number of commissioned officers in an Indian unit, and the fact that the platoons, etc., are commanded by Viceroy's commissioned officers, it is normal for junior officers to find themselves commanding companies or equivalent units quite early in their service. Extra-regimental employment is also open to officers of the Indian Army, such as staff appointments, service with Frontier Scout Corps, the Indian States' Forces, etc.

The Indian Cadets

Officers have been, and are, provided as follows:—

About 20 years before the war the practice was started of giving Indians commissions in the Indian Army. Indian cadets were sent to the Royal Military College, Sandhurst, for the usual two years' course, after which they were gazetted, and attached in the usual manner to a British battalion in India for a year's training before joining an Indian unit. This scheme came to an end when the next stage began. There are at the present time about 125 of these King's Commissioned Indian officers (K.C.I.O.s) in the Indian Army, and most of them are now majors.

The next stage came about eight years before the war, when it was decided to increase Indianisation by the formation of a completely Indianised Division. An Indian Military College on exactly the same lines as Sandhurst was then formed in India at Dehra Dun, to which large batches of selected cadets were sent for a 2 ½ years' course.

When the rapid expansion of the Indian Army was started, Dehra Dun could not supply the number of officers required, so the O.C.T.U. system was adopted, and emergency commissions granted exactly as in England. Large numbers of Indian cadets are now being trained for commissions in this way.

It is considered essential that there should still be a certain percentage of British officers posted to the Indian Army. In order to provide this quota the War Office has organised a scheme of which the details are laid down in A.C.I. 1734 of 1941, under which emergency commissioned, Territorial Army and Special Reserve subaltern officers of the British Army, and cadets at O.C.T.U.s in England may apply for service with the Indian Army.

India's Other Forces

In addition to the regular Indian Army there are:—

(a) The Indian Territorial Force, of which there was usually one Territorial battalion per infantry regiment. The Territorial battalions have now all been converted into regular active battalions and are employed in rôles for the defence of India.

(b) The Auxiliary Force, India. This is a part-time force

consisting of light horse, artillery, engineer, signals, railway, infantry, machine-gun and armoured car units. Its primary rôle is the maintenance of internal security, should the need arise; and it is, as a rule, embodied only in grave emergency. It is recruited from the domiciled European and Anglo-Indian community, principally business men—planters—railway employees.

(c) The Indian Air Force. The Indian Air Force was constituted shortly before the war, and in the first instance consisted of one army co-operation squadron. It has been considerably expanded and further expansion is projected. The Indian Air Force has been in action in Burma with good results, and has also gained valuable experience on the north-west frontier.

(d) The Indian States Forces. There are in India some 560 Indian States whose rulers own allegiance to and have treaty rights with the British Crown. Certain of these States maintain their own contingents of troops. At the outbreak of war the ruling princes unreservedly offered their forces to the Crown. A considerable proportion of these units has proceeded overseas, and many others are employed in the defence of India.

In recording its services in this war it must be remembered that the Indian Army is only a part of the Army of India, of which the British Army furnishes a considerable proportion. There is no such thing as an entirely Indian formation. British artillery, infantry and signallers all form part of Indian divisions. British W.O.s and N.C.O.s are important components of many ancillary units. The short account below continues therefore the record of a comradeship in arms between the British and Indian soldier which has persisted for over 100 years.

The Record of This War

The Army in India in this war has done far more than carry out its formal commitments. The 4th Indian Division took part in the beginnings of General Wavell's offensive in Cyrenaica, captured 20,000 prisoners in three days, and, with British formations, made short work of Sidi Barrani and its surrounding forts.

The 4th Division was then sent to join the 5th Indian Division in East Africa, where, in January, 1941, they began their joint advance into Eritrea. The storming of the sheer stronghold of Keren on March 27th started the break-up of Mussolini's African Empire. British Somaliland was unobtrusively reoccupied. Abyssinia was cleared of Italian troops. In all these operations Indian formations played a considerable part.

Meanwhile, in Libya, the 3rd Indian Motor Brigade's heroic rearguard action at El Mekili enabled the Commonwealth Forces to reach and hold Tobruk. For five months Indians formed part of its beleaguered garrison. Fresh Indian formations were next called upon to stop the activities of Rashid Ali's Forces in Iraq.

Shortly afterwards Indian troops from the Middle East moved, with British and Free French troops, against the subservient Vichy French in Syria, and earned themselves new distinctions in the actions which led up to the capture of Damascus. There followed for the troops in Iraq the four days' campaign in Persia, where the German Fifth Column had become a menace to British communications with Russia.

Later, the 9th and 11th Indian Divisions were in action throughout the operations in Malaya, and the 17th Indian Division, with other Indian troops already in the country, took part in the fighting all through the Burma campaign.

In the recent operations in Libya and Egypt Indian formations have been continuously and heavily engaged throughout. One brigade took part in the defence of Tobruk and shared the fate of the rest of the garrison. Meantime many other formations stand prepared to resist any attempted aggression against India itself, and new recruits offer themselves for enrolment in greater numbers than can be absorbed.

CURRENT AFFAIRS
No. 109(A), December 1st, 1945

TARGET FOR TO-MORROW

This bulletin sets out in brief compass some of the essential background information about India. It can do no more. Whole books have been written about various aspects of this great subcontinent. But why should we bother about India's problems at all, when we have so many already on our own doorstep? The short answer is that our affairs and her affairs are now inextricably mixed up. We may be proud of the past or we may regret the past, but we cannot deny it, nor escape its consequences, and the fact is that we have been associated with India now for nearly a couple of centuries. Whether we act, or fail to act, stay or withdraw, must influence India's future profoundly. We are also members of a democratic community, whose elected Government is trying to solve the Indian problem. Even if we feel that we have not the knowledge nor capacity to formulate our own solutions, we should at least master the general context, in which Indians will be going to the polls this winter, and in which important and far-reaching decisions will be made in our names.

THE BRITISH OFFER

What, then, is to be done about India? The British Government's declaration of March 11th, 1942, which formed the basis of the Cripps proposals, began as follows:

"The object is the creation of a new Indian union which shall constitute a Dominion, associated with the United Kingdom and the other Dominions by a common allegiance to the Crown, but equal to them in every respect, in no way subordinate in any aspect of its domestic or external affairs."

On February 17th, 1944, Lord Waved declared:

"The desire of the British people, of His Majesty's present

Government, and, I am convinced, of any future Government of the United Kingdom is … to see India a prosperous country, a united country, enjoying complete and unqualified self-government as a willing partner in the British Commonwealth."

The British Government's latest plan for India was outlined by Lord Wavell in a broadcast on the All-India Radio in September, 1945:

"It is the intention of His Majesty's Government," he said, *"to convene as soon as possible a constitution-making body, and as a preliminary step they have authorised me to undertake, immediately after the elections, discussions with representatives of the Legislative Assemblies in the Provinces, to ascertain whether the proposals contained in the 1942 Declaration are acceptable or whether some alternative or modified scheme is preferable.*

"Discussions will also be undertaken with the representatives of Indian States with a view to ascertaining in what way they can best take their part in the constitution-making body. His Majesty's Government are proceeding to the consideration of the content of the treaty which will require to be concluded between Great Britain and India.

"During these preparatory stages, the government of India must be carried on, and urgent economic and social problems must be dealt with. Furthermore, India has to play her full part in working out the new world order. His Majesty's Government have therefore authorised me, as soon as the results of the Provincial elections are published, to take steps to bring into being an Executive Council which will have the support of the main Indian parties."

AN INDIAN ANSWER

It must be added, however, that the Congress leaders do not agree with this policy nor with the view expressed at the conclusion of the article that "before we 'quit India' it is plainly our duty to ensure that there exists a strong and legally constituted Indian Government to which power can be transferred; to withdraw without making such provision would be to invite an outbreak of civil war." It doesn't matter, Mr. Gandhi has said, in one of his past pronouncements.

"Leave India in God's hands, in modern parlance to anarchy, and that anarchy may lead to internecine warfare or to unrestrained dacoities.* From these a true India will arise in place of the false one we see."

More recently Pandit Nehru has said:

"The whole of Asia is now in the ferment of a new spirit of revolt against all types of imperialism, which is sweeping the continent. Domination by the British for 150 years has become intolerable. Indians will not wait for more declarations and more promises from New Delhi and London, but will solve the issue of their freedom themselves."

THE PROBLEM STATED

What is to be the outcome of these dangerously irreconcilable attitudes? Before we can risk even the most tentative conclusions we need to know something of India's history and background. Here are some of the questions to ask your group. How big is India? The size of the population? Indian products and resources? (pages 51–56 and maps and diagrams on pages 54, 55, 67 and 72).† How did we first come to India? The beginning of British civil administration? How is India governed to-day? Progress towards self-government? (pages 58–59). Sum up this section, which should give a picture of a country with a vast population, only a fraction of whom are industrially employed, and to whom we have promised self-government.

---

* Armed robberies.

† Diagrams on pages 55 and 72 are by Pictorial Charts, London.

RACIAL AND RELIGIOUS DIFFERENCES

What, then, are the difficulties? Possibly not everyone knows of the division of India into British India and the indian States. What is the difference (pages 58–60 and map on page 58)? But everyone should have heard of communal differences between Moslems and Hindus. How many are there of each? What do they stand for? Are their differences ineradicable? What is the problem of the untouchables? Then again, it is common knowledge that India is a land of many creeds, languages and races. Can your group name the most substantial of the minorities? Probably not. In that case you must tell them (pages 61–64 and map on page 61). Why have negotiations broken down hitherto? (pages 65–66). Sum up this section, which reveals one basic difficulty and a host of minor ones.

ECONOMICS THE KEY?

Next, the condition of the people. The Indian is poor. Everyone has heard of famine and disease. In more detail has anyone any idea of the infant mortality rate, expectation of life, national income per head in India? How do the majority of Indians live? (pages 66–71). What is the root cause of this problem? The obvious answer is the right one, low productivity; and with it the customary but tragic by-products—lack of education and ill-health, ignorance and prejudice. But what causes low productivity? Lack of education and ill-health, ignorance and prejudice. It's the old vicious circle again. In any case there is too dense a population for a predominantly agricultural country. What is the answer? Industrialisation (pages 71–73). Sum up once more.

But what is all this to do with us? This is where we come in. Either your group can discuss the solution to the Indian problem in another session, or you can send them away with a question in their minds and some knowledge with which to judge future events.

ALL PART OF THE ABCA SERVICE

Past ABCA material which can be used to amplify or illustrate the material in this bulletin includes: *Current Affairs* No. 19 "My Mission to India," by Sir Stafford Cripps. *Map Review* No. 70 "India and her fighting men." *ABCA Exhibitions* No. 185 "India Looks Ahead" and No. 220 "Indian Education." *ABCA Films* C.7034 "Arms from India" (1941, Approximate showing time 11 mins.): B/C 7511, "Indian Crisis" (1942, 19 mins.); B/C 7512, "India at War" (1942, 19 mins.). This bulletin concludes a series on the British Commonwealth and Empire. No. 84 "Men from the Dominions," No. 89 "New Zealand," No. 91 "Australia," No. 95 "Canada," No. 107(A) "Colonies," No. 108(A) "South Africa." Those using this series for reference should note two errors:—
No. 95. Diagram on page 5. For "Montreal" read "Toronto."
No. 108(A). Page 2. For "independent" read "not independent."

Indian Background

by Captain Peter Wright, R.A.

Geography

IT is not easy for the Englishman, used to living in a small island, to adjust his mind to the size of the Indian sub-continent with an area nearly 18 times that of Great Britain and a population of just under 400 millions. It is as far from Cape Comorin to the Khyber as it is from London to Alexandria. Or to look at it from the traveller's point of view—if you catch the "Mail" at Victoria Terminus, Bombay, at tea-time on Saturday, you can expect to arrive in Calcutta about 11 o'clock on Monday morning, after a journey of over 1,200 miles. So large an expanse of territory naturally exhibits a wide variety of scenery and climate, which is inevitably to some extent reflected in the habits and character-istics of the people; yet one of the strange things about India is not so much its diversity, which one expects, but the fact that in spite of this diversity the basic social and economic problems are everywhere the same.

To readers of Kipling the word "India" may conjure up pictures of wild, rock-strewn hills on the North-west Frontier, or of a land covered in dense tropical jungle, into which only the most intrepid adventurer dare penetrate. But neither is typical of the country. Fewer than 1 per cent. of India's millions live on the Frontier, and dense jungle is so scarce that much of the Army's training for operations in northern Burma had to be conducted in a region of thorny scrub, with the result that one division coined the phrase "J.E.W.T."— Jungle Exercises Without Trees. There can be few parts of the world where it is so difficult to find solitude; go where one may, there always seems to be someone else about, and even in the remotest spots a head will suddenly pop up from behind a bush or the sound of a woodman's axe come ringing through the air. It remains none the less true that roughly one-ninth of British-India is designated as forest and that less than half is suitable for cultivation.

Although Cherrapunji, in Assam, enjoys the doubtful distinction of having the heaviest recorded rainfall in the world (over 400 inches a year), water is a pressing problem in most parts of India. Almost the whole of the annual rainfall occurs during the months of June, July, August and September, and for the remainder of the year the people are engaged in the constant toil of providing water for their crops and their animals until the coming of the next monsoon. From March to May the landscape extends parched and brown beneath the scorching sun, thick dust lies over the cracked earth and rises in clouds from the roads, broad rivers have shrunk to small streams trickling through an expanse of sand, and streams have disappeared altogether leaving only dried-up nullahs. Irrigation works are an important feature of Indian agriculture, ranging as they do from the giant Sukkur barrage on the Indus to the primitive bullock-driven water wheel, but that there is still wide scope for further development is shown by the fact that in 1938–9 roughly three-quarters of the land under cultivation in British India was without irrigation of any sort. It is in the North that the most fertile and populous regions are to be found, for they are able to draw on the reservoirs of the Himalayas, whose waters are carried down to the plains by a series of great rivers.

Occupations of the people

Geographically, India south of the Himalayas can be divided into two main areas, the broad plains of the North and the arid, triangular plateau known as the Deccan, which occupies the greater part of the V-shaped peninsula. The northern provinces of Bengal, Bihar, the United Provinces and the Punjab occupy less than one-quarter of India, yet they contain nearly half the total population, and in some districts there are as many as 900 inhabitants to the square mile, compared with an average of little over 200 for the whole country. The main occupation of the peoples of India is the production of food, for the peasants are largely dependent for the means of subsistence upon what they grow themselves. In 1941, 339 millions (87 per cent. of the whole population) were living in villages, and the great majority of these were engaged in agriculture. Rice is the most important foodstuff with a total yield in 1940–1 of over 22 million tons: wheat and millets are next with about 10 million tons each. Important crops not designed for immediate local consumption include oilseeds, cotton, jute and sugar-cane; tea, coffee and tobacco give a small but valuable yield. Jute is grown mainly in Bengal, sugar in the United Provinces and Bihar, and tea in Assam and Northern Bengal.

The natural resources of India have not yet been fully explored, for no complete geological survey has ever been made. Rich iron deposits exist in Bihar and have been used by the great Tata plant

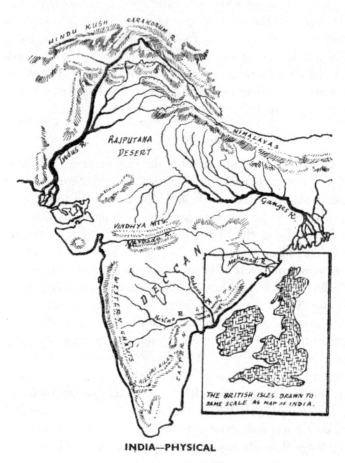

INDIA—PHYSICAL

at Jamshedpur, the largest iron and steel works in the British Empire with an annual production of nearly two million tons of steel and over a million tons of pig-iron. Ninety per cent. of India's coal is derived from a single coalfield in Bihar and Orissa: in 1938 the output was over 28 million tons. Oil-fields are in production in Assam, but their output is very small: before the

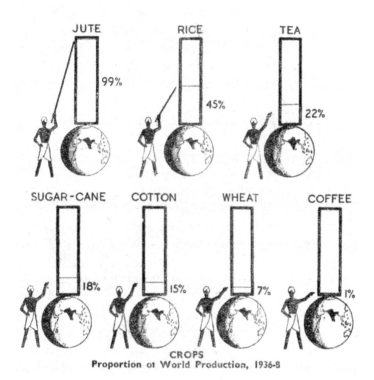

CROPS
Proportion of World Production, 1936-8

war India obtained most of her oil from Burma. The Kolar gold-fields in Mysore yield over 300,000 ounces annually. India also produces about one-quarter of the world's mica, nearly one-fifth of its manganese, and small quantities of monazite and tungsten. Jute and cotton manufactures play an important part in India's economy and have largely contributed to the prosperity of the two great cities of Calcutta (pop., in 1941, 2 millions) and Bombay (1½ millions). Yet in the whole country less than 5 per cent. of the working population are employed in industry, and while there were during the war concerns engaged in the production of such things as field-guns, rifles, shells, motor-tyres and bicycles, in the construction of minesweepers and sloops, and in the repair of aircraft, there is not a single factory capable of turning out a motor-car, a wireless set or a refrigerator. Output of electric power during the whole of 1943 was equivalent to a week's output in the United States, and consumption per head was only 1 per cent. of that in the U.K.

History in outline

The great Himalayan range, which extends from Kashmir to the Burma border, emphasises the geographical unity of India and has helped to isolate the country from contacts with the rest of Asia, but the mountains on the N.W. frontier have never proved an insuperable barrier to the movement of armies, and it is from this direction that the successive land invasions of India have come.

From prehistoric times down to the British conquest a series of invaders swept down through the passes of the North-West to settle in the plains, bringing with them their own customs, religions, and languages. The great variety of physical types to be found in India is the result of this steady infusion of new peoples. S. India, cut off by the Vindhya mountains from the northern plains, was least affected by foreign penetration, and the present-day inhabitants are the direct descendants of the Dravidian aboriginals; in Tamil and Telegu they have retained distinct languages of their own. Hinduism, to-day the religion of two-thirds of the population, may be traced in its origins to the prehistoric Aryan invaders, but Mohammedanism was introduced much later and first exercised wide influence during the Mogul Empire, which was founded in 1526 and was later extended to cover most parts of the peninsula.

The collapse of this empire at the beginning of the eighteenth century prepared the way for the British conquest. The Mahrattas in the west, the Rajputs on the fringes of the Sind desert and the

Sikhs in the Punjab asserted their independence, while further to the south the Mogul Viceroy of the Deccan established his own kingdom in Hyderabad, which has since developed into the largest and wealthiest of the native states. The servants of the East India Company were thus enabled by exploiting one faction against the other to conquer each in turn and to impose their rule upon a weak and divided country.

The British were not the only European power interested in India. The voyage of Vasco de Gama at the end of the fifteenth century first brought the Portuguese to India, and Portugal still retains small colonies on the west coast at Goa, Daman and Diu. France had also staked a claim to an Indian Empire, but as a result of a series of defeats sustained in the middle of the eighteenth century, her possessions in the peninsula were confined to a few small trading posts, which remain French to this day.

The modern political and administrative structure of India was not created overnight, but was evolved gradually as more and more of the country was brought under British control, and provision had to be made for its government. The conquest of India was never planned in Westminster as a deliberate policy, but arose piecemeal out of the activities of a trading company. It was a junior clerk of the East India Company, Robert Clive, who, in 1757, at the battle of Plassey, laid the foundations of British power in India by acquiring control over the province of Bengal. The pacification of further territories was carried out by Clive's successors with the object of advancing the company's trade and establishing the conditions of law and order, which were indispensable to commercial prosperity. By the middle of the nineteenth century the whole of what is now British India had been won for the company, but it was not until after the Mutiny of 1857 that the British Government finally took over the administration.

British India to-day

British India comprises 11 provinces with a total population of nearly 300 millions. The tasks of government are divided between the centre and the provinces in accordance with successive Acts of Parliament; broadly speaking, the centre is responsible for external relations, defence, customs, income-tax, currency,

INDIA—POLITICAL

railways and other matters relating to India as a whole, while the remaining subjects are dealt with by the provincial governments. The Central Government is situated at New Delhi and consists of the Viceroy and an Executive Council, who together form "the Governor-General in Council" and are responsible to the Secretary of State for India and through him to Parliament. The Executive Council is at present composed of four Europeans and ten Indians. There is also in New Delhi a Central Legislature composed of the Council of State and the Legislative Assembly, a majority of both houses being elected on a restricted franchise. Members can initiate legislation and amend or reject Government Bills, but the Governor-General in Council retains a power of veto over the decisions of the Legislature.

Provision was made in the 1935 Act of Parliament for responsible government both at the centre and in the provinces, but the Act has only been applied in the provinces, where in 1937 ministries took office and remained in power until the outbreak of war. As a result of the resignation of the eight Congress ministries in the autumn of 1939, the 1935 Constitution had to be suspended in the provinces concerned, and the government has since been carried on by the Governors and their advisers. We must not, however, forget that for two years responsible self-government was practised in the provinces of British India; it is true that the Governors retained the power of veto, but this was seldom used.

The Civil Service

Meanwhile the day-to-day administration of the country has continued throughout in the hands of the Indian Civil Service, a body of public servants recruited by competitive examination, who perform a variety of important duties as District Magistrates, Collectors, Sessions Judges, Commissioners, and members of the Government Secretariats. Allied to the I.C.S. are the technical services connected with public health, civil engineering, irrigation, forestry and so forth. Each province has its own police force, which draws its officers from the Indian Police Service. The process of Indianising these Government services has been in operation for many years and has made considerable headway. More than half the 1,189 members of the I.C.S. are Indians, and a majority of the new recruits are being drawn from the country. Most of the senior police officers are still British, but the junior posts are being increasingly filled by Indians. In all out of roughly 4,000 posts, which constitute the highest grade of the public services, nearly 2,200 are occupied by Indians; the composition of the lower grades has always been overwhelmingly Indian in character. The number of Indian officers holding the King's Commission is about 11,000; there are also the Viceroy's Commissioned Officers, who have in the past been the backbone of the Indian Army.

The Indian States

A large part of India, amounting in area to about 45 per cent. of the whole and containing roughly 100 million inhabitants, is still governed by Indian princes, whose sovereignty has been recognised in separate treaties concluded by each with the Paramount Power. The latter has an overriding responsibility for external relations and defence, and reserves to itself the right to interfere in the internal affairs of a State in the event of gross misgovernment; subject, however, to these limitations each of the princes is master in his own house and exercises autocratic powers over his subjects. Although the total number of Indian States is over 550, only 20 or 30 of these are of real significance. The most important is Hyderabad, a predominantly Hindu state governed by a Moslem ruler, with an area almost as large as Great Britain, a railway system of its own and a population of 16 millions. In Kashmir, famed for the beauty of its scenery, the position is reversed, and we find a Hindu prince, whose four million subjects are mainly Moslems. One should beware of easy generalisations about the backwardness of the Indian States. In some of the smaller ones it is doubtless true that progress has been limited; on the other hand, Hyderabad, Baroda, and Mysore, the latter with its great hydro-electric power station on the river Cauvery, its extensive irrigation system and its modern hospitals, have set an example in economic development to the whole of India.

The communal problem

Can India be regarded as a single nation? Hindus generally argue that it can: on the other hand, Mr. Jinnah, leader of the Moslem League, claims that it is not one nation, but two, and that this duality, based on religious differences, should be recognised by the creation of two separate states—Hindustan and Pakistan. In one sense neither is right, for many more than two races and

Territories claimed by advocates of Pakistan

THE MOSLEM CLAIM

religions are represented in the peninsula. But it is true that the Hindus (255 millions) and the Moslems (94 millions) are by far the largest communities and that their differences constitute the most formidable obstacle to Indian unity. The Moslems live mainly in the north, where they include most of the population of Sind, the North-West Frontier Province, and Kashmir, and rather more than half that of the Punjab and Bengal. The Moslem community is not, however, concentrated into a compact geographical region, but is inextricably mingled with the rest or the population. It would, therefore, be impracticable to concede the League's demands for Pakistan without including within its boundaries a Hindu population of not less than 40 millions. A further difficulty arises out of the fact that Bengal is separated by a large non-Moslem area from the Punjab and the other provinces, which Mr. Jinnah wishes to include in Pakistan.

It is impossible to understand Indian problems unless one appreciates the extent to which religious issues pervade the everyday life of the people. A man's activities are regulated in accordance with the elaborate code of conduct appropriate to his faith. One need only go back a few hundred years in the history of our own or any other European country to realise that under such conditions a spirit of compromise and toleration is seldom achieved. India is no exception. Communal riots have long been a regular feature of Indian life, and between September, 1939, and December, 1942, alone accounted for the deaths of nearly 500 persons and injuries to 2,000 more. The cause of the disturbance is usually some seemingly trivial event—perhaps a Moslem has sacrificed a cow, an animal sacred to the Hindu, or else a Hindu procession has played music before a mosque. Amongst the educated classes the religious conflict finds expression in bitter disputes over the allocation of government posts or in violent political disagreement. We must not, however, jump to the other extreme of supposing that communal discord is necessarily ineradicable. Urdu, the lingua franca of North and Central India, is itself the product of a fusion of Hindu and Moslem culture. For months on end members of the two communities will live peacefully together in the same towns and villages. It is, moreover, arguable that communal differences have been unnaturally accentuated by the electoral system, by which Hindus and Moslems form separate constituencies; this was introduced in 1919 at the insistence of the Moslems.

Hindu society

Of Hinduism it has been said that it "is not only a religion, it is an all-embracing social system which has no parallel in any other country."* The learned mystic may find in it a sublime conception of philosophical detachment and the abnegation of worldly desires, but to the superstitious and illiterate masses it means something quite different—the uncomprehending worship of stone idols and the spirits that dwell in sacred trees, the propitiation of the awesome deities, who can give or withhold the means of life, and a terrified obedience to the laws of the Brahman priesthood. Hindu society still attaches great importance to the caste system, with its ban on intermarriage, and to elaborate rules about food. Modern Hindu thinking reveals a conflict between those, who wish to maintain intact the traditional structure and ritual of Hinduism, and those, who believe that they must be largely swept away, if India is to adapt herself successfully to the needs of the 20th century. The former school of thought is represented by an organisation known as the Hindu Mahasaba, whereas the latter numbers many advocates in the ranks of the Congress Party.

The most acute of all the problems raised by the caste system is the fate of the 50 million "untouchables"—now known officially as the Scheduled Castes. Belonging to no recognised caste, regarded as unclean by orthodox Hindus, often debarred from admission to the schools and temples of their religion, these unfortunates are condemned by the circumstances of their birth to a position of permanent social inferiority. They are expected to perform the menial occupations, which would be degrading to the caste Hindu, and though their leader, Dr. Ambedkar, has risen to

---

* Lady Hartog. *India in Outline*. (Cambridge University Press).

be Labour Member of the Viceroy's Executive Council, his touch would still be considered to defile a Brahman. Untouchables are to be found all over India sweeping the streets, making leather goods and working in the factories: a high proportion live in the South, where many thousands have been converted to Christianity. Although nominally Hindus, they form a distinct community with an outlook of their own.

The minorities

Brief mention must be made of the other minority communities. The most compact and highly organised are the six million Sikhs, whose home is in the Punjab. They were originally Hindus, but in the 16th century they founded a sect of their own and later set up an independent kingdom. They have no caste and do not smoke or cut their hair. Their martial traditions have been strengthened by fine service rendered in the Indian army in this war and the last, and they are certainly a power that must be reckoned with in any future political settlement, for their leaders have repeatedly declared that they will not submit to Hindu or Moslem rule. The number of Christians in India is more than seven millions. Mission societies have been active during the last 150 years, particularly in the South, and have offered opportunities of education to thousands, who would have otherwise had none; it is no coincidence that the struggle against illiteracy has made most progress in the state of Travancore, where Christians comprise a third of the population of six millions. Included in the Christian total are the European and Anglo-Indian communities: the 1941 census gives them as 135,000 and 140,000 respectively, but the figure for Europeans is misleading, as nearly half were British troops. Another small but highly influential community is the Parsees (115,000), who came originally from Persia. The largest Parsee settlement is in Bombay, where they have won for themselves a leading place in industry and commerce; the best known Parsees are probably the Tata family, whose interests include the great steelworks at Jamshedpur (also called Tatanagar), an airways company and the famous Taj Mahal hotel in Bombay. Other communities accorded a special mention in the census are the Jains (1½ millions) and the Buddhists (232,000)—the former are a sect of Hindus, to whom all forms of life are sacred; the latter are the followers of Gautama Buddha, who was born in northern India about 560 b.c. Buddhism has exerted a profound influence in Indian life, but as a religion it was largely absorbed in Hinduism and survives to-day only in certain hill districts in the North.

Indian Nationalism

In August, 1917, the Secretary of State for India, Mr. Montagu, outlined a new British policy in a declaration, in which he spoke of "the increasing association of Indians in every branch of the administration, and the gradual development of self-governing institutions with a view to the progressive realisation of responsible government in India as an integral part of the Empire." This declaration was the foundation of the subsequent political reforms culminating in the Act of 1935. But "gradual development" did not satisfy the Indian Nationalists. They demanded immediate independence and set about

rousing the masses against British rule. The Congress Party became under Mr. Gandhi's leadership the champion of the nationalist cause. In 1921, following the introduction of the Montagu-Chelmsford reforms, which were the first instalment of the policy announced in 1917, Gandhi organised a nation-wide civil disobedience campaign and inaugurated a career of opposition to the government, which found its most recent expression in the Congress disturbances of August, 1942.

The Congress Party is to-day the most powerful political organisation in India; at the provincial elections of 1937 it obtained a majority in seven out of the 11 provinces. It should be borne in mind however that the electorate was restricted on a property basis to 11 per cent. of the population,* and it is uncertain to what extent the Congress attitude is consciously shared by the people as a whole—it must, indeed, be considered doubtful whether uneducated peasants are capable of understanding the issues involved. Moreover, in spite of the fact that at the moment its president happens to be a Moslem, Dr. Azad, Congress is predominantly a Hindu party, and its claim to speak for the other communities is challenged both by the Moslem League and by the political leaders of the Scheduled Castes. That the minority parties are still actuated by fear of Hindu domination has been proved by the breakdown of the Gandhi-Jinnah talks in October, 1944, and by the failure of the Simla negotiations in July of this year.

The condition of the people

The attention of the outside world tends to be focused on the political scene to the exclusion of all else. Yet India's basic problem is not political in the narrow sense of the word, but economic—how to improve the living conditions of the people. Figures alone cannot convey an idea of the appalling poverty of the country. The Bengal famine in 1943, which is believed to have caused 1½ million deaths, created a world sensation, but little is known outside India of the constant toll of life that is being taken by malnutrition and disease. The infant mortality rate is four times as high as in England; expectation of life at birth is about 27 years or well under half that in England; deaths due to malaria alone are estimated at over a million a year, and other preventable diseases, such as small-pox, typhoid, dysentery, cholera and bubonic plague, are daily claiming hundreds of victims, while the ravages of hookworm are another grave menace to the

---

* A similar register will be used for the coming provincial elections.

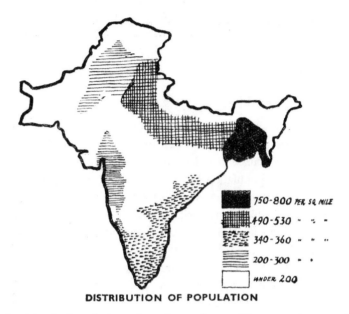

DISTRIBUTION OF POPULATION

(legend)
750-800 PER SQ. MILE
490-530 " " "
340-360 " " "
200-300 " "
UNDER 200

health of a largely bare-footed population. The typical peasant's diet consists almost entirely of cereals and is sadly deficient in proteins, vitamins and calcium; he seldom eats fruit or vegetables, and milk is drunk only in small quantities. Calculations for the year 1931 showed that the annual national income worked out at under £5 per head, that was about one-fifteenth of the figure for Britain and less than one-quarter of that for Japan. Although India is one of the world's largest manufacturers of cotton goods, the consumption per head in 1929 was less than 40 per cent. of the world average. Acute overcrowding exists in towns and villages alike. The normal village house, consisting of a dark one- or two-roomed mud hut perhaps 20 ft. square, has to serve as living accommodation for five or six persons, and here the whole family must cook, eat and sleep together, often with cows and chickens for company. In industrial areas in Bombay before the war the average floor space per person was found to be less than 30 sq. ft. It is a common sight to see coolies and beggars spending the night on railway platforms and street pavements for want of anywhere else to sleep, or because their rooms are overcrowded.

Agricultural problems

One of the root causes of the problem is the fact that the rapid expansion of population has not been accompanied by a corresponding increase in agricultural production. In the 20 years 1921–1941 the population increased from 306 millions to 389 millions, but over the same period the total yield of cereals rose only from 45 to 46 million tons. Birth control is practically unknown, and the birth rate for 1939 was more than double that in Britain. Although a start was made in 1904 with the establishment by the Government of the first Agricultural Research Institute, modern methods of scientific agriculture have as yet made an impression only in a comparatively few regions. Mechanisation is unknown, the peasant continuing to till his soil and harvest his crop by hand with the aid of his family and his one or two bullocks. Co-operative methods, however, are making headway, and in 1942 there were 126,000 agricultural societies with a membership of 4 ½ millions. Figures of yield per acre of some basic crops show that India is far behind other countries in this respect: the yield of rice, for example, is one-third of that in the U.S.A. and of cotton one-half. Agricultural development has been hindered by the Hindu system of inheritance, as a result of which the average holding consists of two or three acres scattered in tiny allotments all over the village. Other social and religious customs have contributed to rural poverty. Because the cow is sacred to the Hindus, cattle have been allowed to multiply without restraint. To-day more than a third of all the cattle in the world are to be found in India, but large numbers of these are quite useless, for they may not be used

A TYPICAL VILLAGE SCENE

as food, and so they merely eat up fodder which might otherwise keep the remainder in good condition. The loss involved in maintaining these useless animals has been estimated as equivalent to four times the entire land revenue of the country. The system of land tenure varies in different parts of the country; in the northern provinces the peasant usually rents his land from a big landowner (*Zemindar*), in the south he more often owns the land himself. But in either case a tax is paid to the Government under the system of land revenue originally instituted by the Moguls. This system has been carried on by the British, and land revenue is the main source of income of the provincial governments. A further drain on the peasant's meagre resources arises out of debts contracted with local moneylenders (*Banias*) to tide over a bad harvest or to provide for a marriage feast, which custom dictates should be on a lavish scale out of all proportion to the means of the family. Rural indebtedness is a big problem all over India amounting before the war to something like £900 million.

Education and health

If India is to make any real progress towards economic prosperity or democratic self-government, one of the first things that must be done is to bring education to the people. For the illiterate peasant is capable of understanding neither the methods of scientific cultivation nor the responsibilities of the voter. In 1941 81 per cent. of the male and 95 per cent. of the female population were classified as illiterate. Only in a very few districts is elementary education compulsory and in many it is non-existent; over two-thirds of the villages in the country have no school at all. Gradual progress is, however, being made, as is shown by the fact that the percentage of literates rose from 7 per cent. in 1931 to 12 per cent. in 1941. The difference between the sexes is attributable to the inferior social status accorded to women by Hindus and Moslems alike. Higher education has been provided on a much more adequate scale. There are 19 universities in India with about 180,000 students, of whom 15,000 are women; English is the usual language of instruction. Unfortunately, however, the careers, which seem most attractive to the educated Indians, the legal profession, for example, are seldom those of most value to the country, and the problem of the "failed B.A. Calcutta" is only one instance of the way in which the educational system is ill adjusted to the requirements of an undeveloped society.

Lack of education is also one of the main obstacles to the raising of health standards. The problem is not merely one of providing the necessary facilities—doctors, hospitals, dispensaries, sanitation and so on—but of persuading the people to use them. It needs more than an up-to-date public lavatory in every village to induce the peasants to abandon the unhygienic habits of centuries. Malaria treatment and small-pox vaccine may be available round the corner, but how can a man hope by such magic to rid himself of the visitations of Providence? The refusal to accept the inventions of the 20th century is strikingly demonstrated by the popularity of the cult of Ayurvedic medicine, which is based on the practice and experience of bygone ages.

In spite, however, of these psychological handicaps there is still enormous scope for improvement on the material side. In 1939 India had one hospital bed to every 4,000 people, one doctor to every 9,000 and one trained nurse to every 86,000; corresponding figures for England were (to the nearest hundred) 200, 800 and 400. Only 253 out of 1,471 towns in British India have a protected water supply— in the villages sanitation of any sort is unknown, and the inhabitants drink out of the same tank, in which they wash their clothes, bathe their bodies and water their buffaloes. The Indian Medical Service has done fine work, particularly in the field of research (it was one of its officers, Sir Ronald Ross, who discovered the source of malaria infection), but it has been handicapped by limited resources. The situation calls for greatly increased government expenditure on the health services coupled with extensive propaganda to encourage the use of existing facilities.

The future of industry

In view of the fact that the rural population is too large for the land to support even with the most advanced methods of cultivation, the desired increase in the standard of living can only be brought about by industrial development. In 1939 there were in the whole of India only 10,466 industrial concerns (as defined in the Factory Acts), and these employed fewer than 1½ million workers, the remainder of the industrial population being mainly engaged in domestic handicrafts. A division of opinion exists amongst educated Indians as to the kind of industrial development that is desirable. Gandhi himself has consistently favoured the small village industries, of which the *charka* or handloom is symbolic, but there has lately been a growing movement for

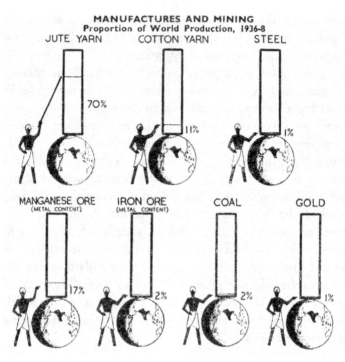

MANUFACTURES AND MINING
Proportion of World Production, 1936-8

JUTE YARN   COTTON YARN   STEEL

70%

11%

1%

MANGANESE ORE   IRON ORE   COAL   GOLD
(METAL CONTENT)   (METAL CONTENT)

17%

2%

2%

1%

the expansion of heavy machine industry. In January, 1944, a group of Bombay industrialists published "A Plan of Economic Development for India." This envisages the expenditure of a sum of £7,500 million over a period of 10 years—and nearly half this amount (£3,360 million) is earmarked for industrial expansion, priority being given to the basic industries such as electric power, iron and steel, chemicals, and cement. It is suggested that economic conditions in India to-day are comparable to those in Russia after the last war and that the development of cheap hydro-electric power, to which the country is ideally suited, must be the foundation of subsequent prosperity. Great importance is also attached in this plan to the development of communications. The existing 41,000 miles of railways (now almost entirely under

State control) and 300,000 miles of road, of which only 74,000 are metalled, would need in the opinion of the authors of the plan to be increased by 50 per cent. and 100 per cent. respectively to cope with the greater traffic resulting from the suggested expansion of industry.

How it concerns us

What is all this to do with us? The answer is that our long association with India has profoundly affected the course of her development and imposes upon us an obligation to assist her not only to achieve self-government, but also to promote the material welfare of her people. This obligation has been emphasised by the magnificent services rendered to the allied cause during the war by the Indian army. British rule has conferred undoubted benefits, but might not equal or even greater advantages have been gained without our intervention? Nor can it be denied that the introduction of western conceptions of justice and education have created new problems for an oriental people. It is no longer true—if, indeed, it ever was—that India's resources are being drained to fill our pockets. The transfer of capital from British to Indian hands has been accelerated by the war, and India has accumulated large sterling assets. But a consideration for India's welfare is alone sufficient to explain why the British Government has not yet been able to implement the offer of independence contained in the Cripps proposals. Before we "quit India," it is plainly our duty to ensure that there exists a strong and legally constituted Indian Government, to which power can be transferred; to withdraw without making such provision would be to invite an outbreak of civil war.

OTHER TITLES IN THIS SERIES

Other books of Army Bureau of Current Affairs material:—